APR 2 1 2015

creepy creatures

Published by Creative Education
P.O. Box 227, Mankato, Minnesota 56002
Creative Education is an imprint of
The Creative Company
www.thecreativecompany.us

Design by Ellen Huber
Production by Chelsey Luther
Art direction by Rita Marshall
Printed in the United States of America

Photographs by Dreamstime (Basphoto, Fscotto74, Isselee, Lantapix), Getty Images (Sherman/Three Lions), iStockphoto (Evgeniy Ayupov, Eric Isselée, spxChrome, TommyIX), Photo Researchers (Eye of Science/Science Source), Shutterstock (Lindsey Eltinge, Hal_P, Shadrina Irina, Cosmin Manci, MustafaNC, Fedorov Oleksiy, Sarah2, WilleeCole, Joanna Zopoth-Lipiejko), SuperStock (Animals Animals, Minden Pictures, NHPA)

Library of Congress Cataloging-in-Publication Data
Bodden, Valerie.
Fleas / Valerie Bodden.
p. cm. — (Creepy creatures)
Summary: A basic introduction to fleas, examining where they live, how they grow, what they eat, and the unique traits that help to define them, such as their ability to jump great distances.
ISBN 978-1-60818-355-5
1. Fleas—Juvenile literature. I. Title. II. Series: Bodden, Valerie. Creepy creatures.
QL599.5.B63 2014
595.77′5—dc23   2013009795

First Edition
9 8 7 6 5 4 3 2 1

CONTENTS

fleas

VALERIE BODDEN

CREATIVE C EDUCATION

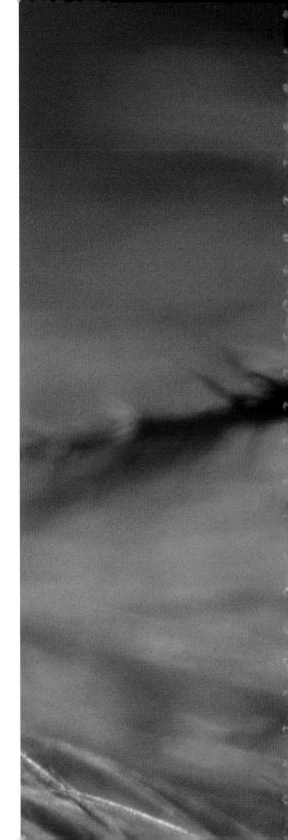

You are petting your dog. Suddenly he begins to scratch his neck. You look closer to see what is making him itch. Something is stuck to his skin.

It is a flea!

Fleas are insects. They have three body parts and six legs. Their two back legs are long to help them jump. Fleas have two **antennae** (*an-TEH-nee*). They have a straw-shaped mouthpart. Fleas do not have wings.

Since fleas do not have wings, they use strong back legs to jump

Most fleas are reddish brown. The smallest fleas are smaller than the period at the end of this sentence. The biggest fleas are about the size of your thumbnail.

Fleas are often too small to see, but they can be felt

There are about 2,380 kinds of fleas. The dog flea is found on dogs. Cat fleas live on cats. About 700 years ago, rat fleas spread a disease called plague (*PLAYG*) to people. Millions of people died.

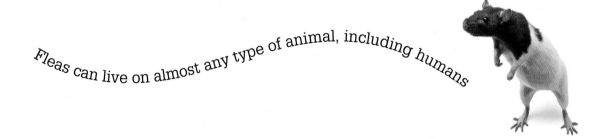

Fleas can live on almost any type of animal, including humans

Monkeys regularly comb through their hair to get rid of fleas

Fleas live on animals around the world. The animals they live on are called hosts. Most fleas live on **mammals**. But some live on birds. Fleas have to watch out for their host animal's claws, teeth, or beaks.

Fleas lay eggs on their host or in its nest. When a flea egg hatches, a **larva** comes out. The larva grows too big for its skin. It **molts** two times. Then the larva becomes a **pupa**. It spins a silk covering called a cocoon around itself. When it comes out of the cocoon, it is an adult. Most adult fleas live a few months. Some live up to a year.

A female flea can lay up to 2,000 eggs in her lifetime

A flea larva is blind and likes to stay in dark places

A female flea can eat 15 times her body weight in 1 day

Flea larvae eat dead skin, feathers, or hair.
Adult fleas are parasites. They live
on their animal hosts and take
food from them in the
form of blood.

Fleas are great jumpers. Some fleas can jump more than a foot (30.5 cm)! Fleas are tough, too. A hard shell covers their flat bodies. This makes them hard to crush.

Cat fleas can be hard to find unless they jump up high

The first flea circus was started in England in the 1830s

In some places, people used to keep flea circuses. They would tie tiny carts to the fleas. People watched the cart-pulling fleas through a magnifying glass. It can be fun to watch these tiny creepy creatures!

Fleas have been on Earth for nearly 100 million years

MAKE A FLEA CIRCUS

You can make your own flea circus using raisins as fleas. Cut some small squares from colored paper. These can be your carts. Glue a piece of string to each cart. Glue the other end of each string to a raisin. Now make your fleas pull the carts!

GLOSSARY

antennae: feelers on the heads of some insects that are used to touch, smell, and taste things

larva: the form some insects and animals take when they hatch from eggs, before changing into their adult form

mammals: animals that have hair or fur and feed their babies with milk

molts: loses a shell or layer of skin and grows a new, larger one

pupa: an insect that is changing from a larva into an adult, usually while inside a covering or case to keep it safe

READ MORE

Huggins-Cooper, Lynn. *Beastly Bugs*. North Mankato, Minn.: Smart Apple Media, 2007.

Twist, Clint. *The Life Cycle of Fleas*. Mankato, Minn.: NewForest Press, 2013.

WEBSITES

Flea Printable Coloring Pages

http://www.kidsuki.com/s/Flea/

Print out pictures of fleas to color.

Kids Health: Hey! A Flea Bit Me!

http://kidshealth.org/kid/ill_injure/bugs/flea.html

Learn what to do if you are bitten by a flea.

INDEX